VICTORIOU

Targeted Healing Scriptures *for* Personal Meditation

VICTORIOUS GRIEF: Targeted Healing Scriptures for Personal Meditation
A Companion Transformative Guide for:
VICTORIOUS GRIEF: God's Realignment for Your New Assignment

Published by:
The Armor of Truth Press
150 Buckeye Drive
Colorado Springs, CO 80919
(562) 799-7710

IMPORTANT ADVICE & LAWYER-PROOFING DISCLAIMER: The Biblical content in this volume is designed to be used in conjunction with its parent/companion volume, *"VICTORIOUS GRIEF: God's Realignment for Your New Assignment."* Even if this volume is used independently of its companion text, the reader can expect significant and transformative changes to occur by allowing the Holy Spirit to turn the printed words on the page into power to heal and establish a more intimate relationship with God the Father, God the Son, and God the Holy Spirit. All content is intended for informational and educational purposes only, and is not in any way a substitute for pastoral, professional or medical care for symptoms related to bereavement, grief and mourning. Always seek appropriate professional and spiritual help in addition to using the content of this book and other Biblical resources. Never delay seeking pastoral, mental health, or medical help due to anything you encounter here. As God says in His Word, "Where there is no counsel, the people fall but in the multitude of counselors there is safety." Proverbs 11:13. The author would also be happy to assist you in finding pastoral or mental health care nearby to you or online, qualified help you can trust — just call the phone number above; we are here for you.

ISBN 979-8-9863794-4-9
Printed and Digitally Produced in the United States of America

WELCOME

To you, our beloved reader . . .

When the Lord first led me to put everything else aside and write "Victorious Grief," it was my heartfelt desire to reach out to those grappling with the overwhelming flood-tide of sorrow and loss. Over time, this journey has been punctuated with amazing stories and serendipities that have only affirmed the profound interconnectedness of our lives and the timeless solace offered by faith—as well as God's perfect timing.

One such divine orchestration involved a beloved friend, whom my wife called her "exterior decorator with the magical hands" — her hairdresser, De. After my beloved bride of 47 years was called to her eternal Home, De started managing my own increasing grays. Each time I sat in her chair, she eagerly asked, "Is your book done yet? I want a copy."

God's timing is impeccable. A mere two weeks after handing her a copy of "Victorious Grief," De faced the crushing loss of her mother, Arlis. Before traveling to the funeral, I offered her several copies for her family, hoping those words would provide some solace and strength. Her daughter, Haley, after reading it, poignantly mentioned, "This book is so helpful, but I think you should tell Dr. Browning that some of us aren't all that familiar with the Bible. So, I suggest he write out all the Scriptures in the book so we could have all of them in one place to meditate on."

Little did Haley know that only a few weeks later, she would say goodbye not only to Grandma, but also to her dear father-in-law, Jeff. Perfect example of the ripple effect of God's lovingkindness and tender mercies with precision timing.

Haley's sweet yet profound suggestion echoed the sentiments of many others. It drove home the realization that, while the book touched upon the key portions of divine wisdom, there was a need for direct access to all the scriptures in simple, easy-to-understand verses all in one place.

Thus, responding to this gentle nudge from the Lord, I decided to curate a collection of scripture as a companion to Victorious Grief. This scripture collection is a carefully chosen ensemble of divine promises, lessons, and assurances. Each scripture is intended to complement the chapters of "Victorious Grief," bridging our earthly understanding and pure heavenly wisdom.

Whether revisiting a particular chapter in "Victorious Grief," or simply seeking a momentary refuge from the peace the Word, this Scripture collection is designed to be your safe harbor light beacon, and the anchor of your soul — even the the storms of mourning and bereavement.

Allow all the truths you discover here to guide, uplift, and remind you of the ever-present love and grace of God that envelopes you, even in your most profound moments of grief.

Lord, shepherd this dear reader into new levels of comfort, hope, inner strength, and a renewed sense of purpose. Help them to behold with an eternal mindset Your path for their future... one moment at a time, one choice at a time.

You'll be amazed how God uses the laser-focused truths in this little book to help you become rooted and grounded in what "future grieving" looks and feels like. As God promises in His Word, "They go from strength to strength...from faith to faith...from glory to glory" (Psalm 84:7 • Romans 1:17 • 2 Corinthians 3:18).

Flip to any page in this book and that is exactly what will happen for you! See for yourself, as you lay a new foundation for the rest, and the best chapter of your life!

With deepest gratitude and blessings,
Dr. Browning

SECTION 1

You're Not Gonna Go
Through This Alone

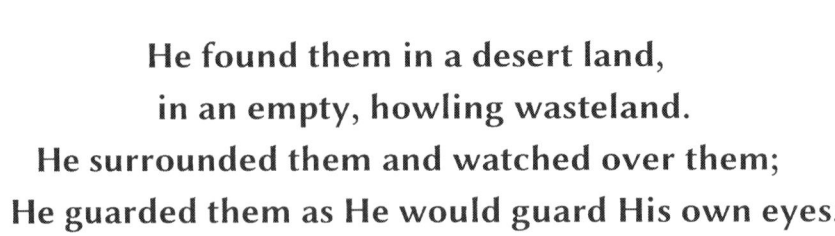

He found them in a desert land,
in an empty, howling wasteland.
He surrounded them and watched over them;
He guarded them as He would guard His own eyes.
— *Deuteronomy 32:10*

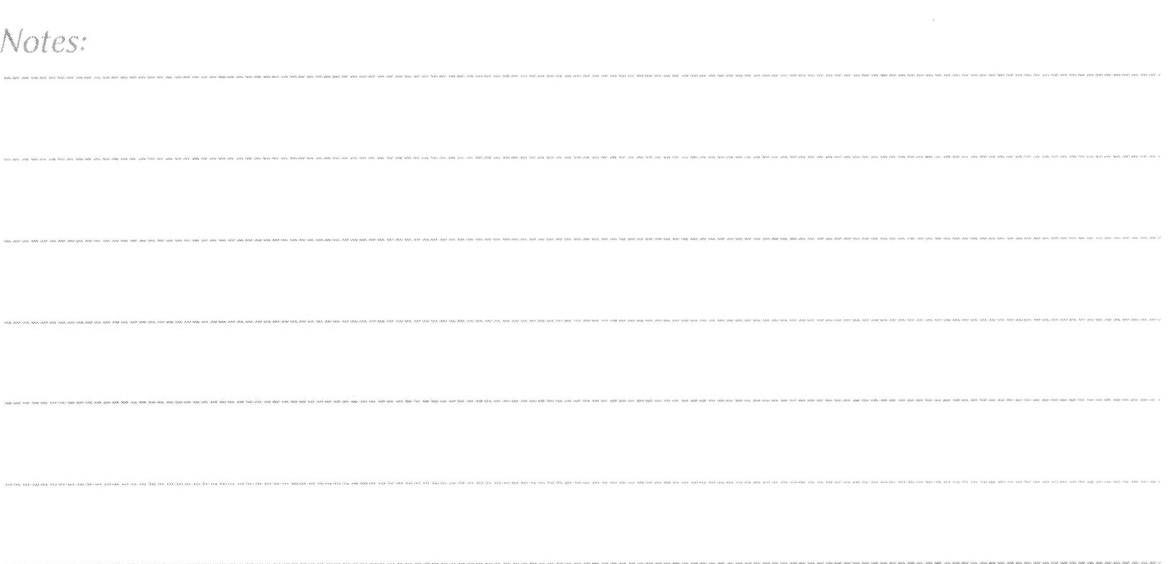

Even when I walk
through the darkest valley,
I will not be afraid,
for You are close beside me.
Your rod and Your staff
protect and comfort me.
— *Psalm 23:4*

Notes:
_____

_____

_____

_____

_____

SECTION 2

*Beyond Thought-Trauma
to Thought-Reversal*

As for me, I look to the Lord for help.
I wait confidently for God to save me,
and my God will certainly hear me.
Do not gloat over me, my enemies!
For though I fall, I will rise again.
Though I sit in darkness,
the Lord will be my light.

— *Micah 7:7-8*

Notes:

SECTION 3

The Mindset-Reset Solution

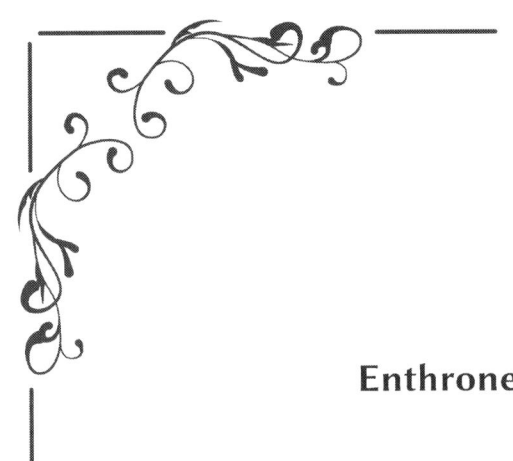

Yet You are holy,
Enthroned on the praises of [Your people].
— *Psalm 22:3*

**He must become greater and greater,
and I must become less and less.**
— *John 3:30*

Notes:

SECTION 4

*Replacing Self's Thoughts
with God's Thoughts*

Throw off your old sinful nature and your former way of life,
which is corrupted by lust and deception.
Instead, let the Spirit renew your thoughts and attitudes.
Put on your new nature, created to be like God
—truly righteous and holy.
— *Ephesians 4:22-24*

But thank God! He gives us victory over sin and death
through our Lord Jesus Christ.
— *1 Corinthians 15:57*

Notes:

SECTION 5

Applying the Mindset-Reset Solution

Trust in the Lord with all your heart;
do not depend on your own understanding.
Seek His will in all you do,
and He will show you which path to take.

— *Proverbs 3:5-6*

Even when I walk
through the darkest valley,
I will not be afraid,
for You are close beside me.
Your rod and Your staff
protect and comfort me.

— *Psalm 23:4*

For we who worship by the Spirit of God
are the ones who are truly circumcised.
We rely on what Christ Jesus has done for us.
We put no confidence in human effort,

— *Philippians 3:3*

And so, dear brothers and sisters,
I plead with you to give your bodies to God
because of all He has done for you.
Let them be a living and holy sacrifice
the kind He will find acceptable.
This is truly the way to worship Him.
Don't copy the behavior and customs of this world,
but let God transform you into a new person
by changing the way you think.
Then you will learn to know God's will for you,
which is good and pleasing and perfect.
— *Romans 12:1-2*

Notes:

SECTION 6

Experiencing the Healing
Power of Proverbs 3:5-6

And you will know the truth, and the truth will set you free...
So if the Son sets you free, you are truly free.
— John 8:32,36

He lifted me out of the pit of despair,
out of the mud and the mire.
He set my feet on solid ground [Rock]
and steadied me as I walked along.
— Psalm 40:2

Notes:

SECTION 7

Letting God Give You the Trust You Lack

I am the Lord, and I do not change.
That is why you descendants of [the carnal] Jacob are not
already destroyed.
— *Malachi 3:6*

Jesus Christ is the same yesterday, today, and forever.
— *Hebrews 13:8*

Look! I stand at the door and knock.
If you hear My voice and open the door,
I will come in, and we will share a meal together as friends.
Those who are victorious will sit with Me on My throne,
just as I was victorious and sat with My Father on His throne.
— *Revelations 3:20-21*

Create in me a clean heart, O God.
Renew a loyal spirit within me.
— *Psalm 51:10*

I am the Lord, and I do not change.
That is why you descendants of [the carnal] Jacob are not
already destroyed.
— *Malachi 3:6*

Look! I stand at the door and knock.
If you hear My voice and open the door,
I will come in, and we will share a meal together as friends.
Those who are victorious will sit with Me on My throne,
just as I was victorious and sat with My Father on His throne.
— *Revelations 3:20-21*

Jesus Christ is the same yesterday, today, and forever.
— *Hebrews 13:8*

If you need wisdom, ask our generous God,
and He will give it to you.
He will not rebuke you for asking.
— *James 1:1-5*

"For I know the plans I have for you," says the Lord.
"They are plans for good and not for disaster,
to give you a future and a hope.
In those days when you pray, I will listen.
If you look for me wholeheartedly, you will find Me.
I will be found by you," says the Lord.
"I will end your captivity and restore your fortunes.
I will gather you out of the nations where I sent you
and will bring you home again to your own land."
— *Jeremiah 29:11-14*

I waited patiently for the Lord to help me,
and He turned to me and heard my cry.
He lifted me out of the pit of despair,
out of the mud and the mire.
He set my feet on solid ground [Rock]
and steadied me as I walked along.
— *Psalm 40:1-2*

This is what the Lord says:
"I will go before you...
and level the mountains.
I will smash down gates of bronze
and cut through bars of iron.
And I will give you treasures hidden in the darkness—
secret riches.
I will do this so you may know that I am the Lord,
the God of Israel, the One who calls you by name."
"And why have I called you for this work?
Why did I call you by name when you did not know Me?
It is for the sake of Jacob my servant,
Israel My chosen one."
— *Isaiah 45:2-4*

Notes:

SECTION 8

The Ever-Present Anchor of Your Soul

This hope is a strong and trustworthy anchor for our souls.
It leads us through the curtain into God's inner sanctuary.
— *Hebrews 6:19*

Don't be afraid, for I am with you.
Don't be discouraged, for I am your God.
I will strengthen you and help you.
I will hold you up with My victorious right hand.

... For I hold you by your right hand —
I, the Lord your God.
And I say to you,
'Don't be afraid. I am here to help you."
— *Isaiah 41:10,13*

God is our refuge and strength,
always ready to help in times of trouble
— *Psalm 46:1*

To all who mourn in Israel,
He will give a crown of beauty for ashes,
a joyous blessing instead of mourning,
festive praise instead of despair.
In their righteousness, they will be like great oaks
that the Lord has planted for His own glory.
— *Isaiah 61:3*

The Lord replied,
"I will personally go with you, Moses,
and I will give you rest—everything will be fine for you."
— *Exodus 33:14*

The high and lofty One who lives in eternity,
the Holy One, says this:
"I live in the high and holy place
with those whose spirits are contrite and humble.
I restore the crushed spirit of the humble
and revive the courage of those with
repentant hearts.
— *Isaiah 57:15*

Since you have been raised to new life with Christ,
set your sights on the realities of heaven,
where Christ sits in the place of honor at God's right hand.
Think about the things of heaven, not the things of earth.
For you died to this life, and your real life is hidden with Christ in God.
— *Colossians 3:1-3*

For He raised us from the dead along with Christ
and seated us with Him in the heavenly realms
because we are united with Christ Jesus.
— *Ephesians 2:6*

Notes:

SECTION 9

Your Loved One –
the Father's Love Gift to Jesus!

Father, I want these whom You have given Me
to be with Me where I am.
Then they can see all the glory You gave Me
because You loved Me even before the world began!
— *John 17:24*

Therefore, let us offer through Jesus
a continual sacrifice of praise to God,
proclaiming our allegiance to His name.
— *Hebrews 13:15*

Let them praise the Lord for His great love
and for the wonderful things He has done for them.
Let them offer sacrifices of thanksgiving
and sing joyfully about His glorious acts.
— *Psalm 107:21,22*

So Christ has truly set us free.
Now make sure that you stay free,
and don't get tied up [entangled] again in slavery to the law.
— *Galatians 5:1*

And you will know the truth,
and the truth will set you free.
So if the Son sets you free,
you are truly free.
— *John 8:32,36*

For the Lord is the Spirit,
and wherever the Spirit of the Lord is,
there is freedom [liberty].
— *2 Corinthians 3:17*

And Nehemiah continued, "Go and celebrate with a feast
of rich foods and sweet drinks, and share gifts of food with people
who have nothing prepared. This is a sacred day before our Lord.
Don't be dejected and sad, for the joy of the Lord is your strength!"
— *Nehemiah 8:10*

Take delight in the Lord,
and He will give you your heart's desires.
— *Psalm 37:4*

Notes:

SECTION 10

*Letting God's Word Guard
and Guide your Heart: Q&A*

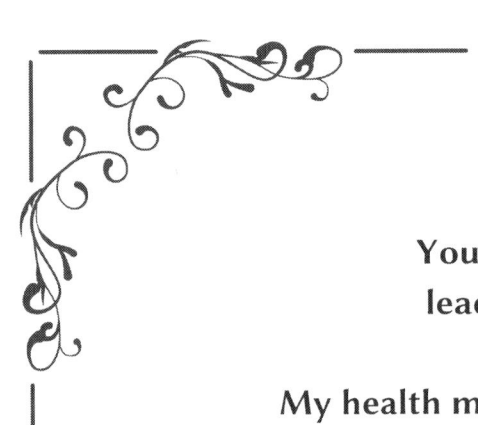

You guide me with Your counsel,
leading me to a glorious destiny.

My health may fail, and my spirit may grow weak,
but God remains the strength of my heart;
He is mine forever.

But as for me, how good it is to be near God!
I have made the Sovereign Lord my shelter,
and I will tell everyone about the wonderful things You do.
— *Psalm 73:24,26,28*

Come close to God, and God will come close to you.
Wash your hands, you sinners; purify your hearts,
for your loyalty is divided between God and the world.
— *James 4:8*

When the Spirit of Truth comes, He will guide you into all truth.
He will not speak on His own but will tell you what He has heard.
He will tell you about the future.
— *John 16:13*

The Spirit alone gives eternal life. Human effort accomplishes nothing.
And the very words I have spoken to you are spirit and life.
— *John 6:63*

"The Spirit of the Lord is upon Me,
for He has anointed Me to bring Good News to the poor.
He has sent Me to proclaim that captives will be released,
that the blind will see,
that the oppressed will be set free,"
— *Luke 4:18*

God blesses those who mourn,
for they will be comforted.
— *Matthew 5:4*

The Lord is close to the brokenhearted;
He rescues those whose spirits are crushed.
— *Psalm 34:18*

"You are worthy, O Lord our God,
to receive glory and honor and power.
For You created all things,
and they exist because You created what You pleased
[and what brings You pleasure.]"
— *Revelation 4:11*

He heals the brokenhearted
and bandages their wounds.
— *Psalm 147:3*

A good reputation is more valuable than costly perfume.
And the day you die is better than the day you are born.
— *Ecclesiastes 7:1*

For we don't live for ourselves or die for ourselves.
If we live, it's to honor the Lord.
And if we die, it's to honor the Lord.
So whether we live or die, we belong to the Lord.
— *Romans 14:7-8*

Precious in the sight of the Lord
is the death of His saints.
— *Psalm 116:15 KJV*

Don't you realize that your body is the temple of the Holy Spirit,
Who lives in you and was given to you by God?
You do not belong to yourself,
for God bought you with a high price.
So you must honor God with your body.
— *1 Corinthians 6:19-20*

He will redeem them from oppression and violence,
for their lives are precious to Him.
— *Psalm 72:14*

Good people pass away;
the godly often die before their time.
But no one seems to care or wonder why.
No one seems to understand
that God is protecting them from the evil to come.
For those who follow godly paths
will rest in peace when they die.
— *Isaiah 57:1-2*
(also, read this in The Living Bible TLB)

So we are always confident, even though we know that
as long as we live in these bodies we are not at home with the Lord.
For we live by believing and not by seeing.
Yes, we are fully confident, and we would rather be away
from these earthly bodies,
for then we will be at home with the Lord.
— *2 Corinthians 5:6-8*

Finally, the poor man died and was carried by the angels
to sit beside Abraham at the heavenly banquet.
The rich man also died and was buried,
— *Luke 16:22*

For I fully expect and hope that I will never be ashamed,
but that I will continue to be bold for Christ,
as I have been in the past. And I trust that my life
will bring honor to Christ, whether I live or die.
For to me, living means living for Christ,
and dying is even better. But if I live, I can do more
fruitful work for Christ [here].
So I really don't know which is better.
I'm torn between two desires: I long to go and be with Christ,
which would be far better for me.
— *Philippians 1:20-23*

Then I saw a new heaven and a new earth, for the old heaven and the old earth
had disappeared. And the sea was also gone. And I saw the holy city, the new
Jerusalem, coming down from God out of heaven like a bride beautifully
dressed for her husband.
I heard a loud shout from the throne, saying, "Look, God's home is now among
His people! He will live with them, and they will be His people. God Himself will
be with them. He will wipe every tear from their eyes, and there will be no more
death or sorrow or crying or pain.
All these things are gone forever."
And the one sitting on the throne said, "Look, I am making everything new!"
And then He said to me, "Write this down, for what I tell you is trustworthy and
true."
And He also said, "It is finished! I am the Alpha and the Omega—the Beginning
and the End.
To all who are thirsty
I will give freely from the springs of the water of life.
All who are victorious will inherit all these blessings,
and I will be their God, and they will be My children."

— *Revelation 21:1-7*

Finally, the poor man died and was carried by the angels
to sit beside Abraham at the heavenly banquet.
The rich man also died and was buried.

— *Luke 16:22*

But we are citizens of heaven, where the Lord Jesus Christ lives.
And we are eagerly waiting for Him to return as our Savior.
He will take our weak mortal bodies and change them
into glorious bodies like His own, using the same power
with which He will bring everything under His control.
— *Philippians 3:20-21*

But they were looking for a better place, a heavenly Homeland.
That is why God is not ashamed to be called their God,
for He has prepared a city for them.
— *Hebrews 11:16*

And I heard a voice from heaven saying,
"Write this down: Blessed are those who die in the Lord
from now on. Yes, says the Spirit, they are blessed indeed,
for they will rest from their hard work; for their good deeds follow
them!"
— *Revelation 14:13*

In the beginning God created the heavens and the earth.
— Genesis 1:1

I am the Lord, and I do not change.
That is why you descendants of Jacob [carnal rebel] are not
already destroyed.
— Malachi 3:6

Jesus Christ is the same yesterday, today, and forever.
— Hebrews 13:8

Don't love money; be satisfied with what you have. For God has said,
"I will never fail you.
I will never abandon you."
So we can say with confidence,
The Lord is my Helper,
so I will have no fear.
What can mere people do to me?
—Hebrews 13:5-6

This is what the Lord says:
"I will go before you...
and level the mountains.
I will smash down gates of bronze
and cut through bars of iron.
And I will give you treasures hidden in the darkness—
secret riches.
I will do this so you may know that I am the Lord,
the God of Israel, the One who calls you by name."
"And why have I called you for this work?
Why did I call you by name when you did not know Me?
It is for the sake of Jacob my servant,
Israel my chosen one."
— Isaiah 45:2-4

Praise the Lord who has given rest to His people...
just as He promised. Not one word has failed of all the
wonderful promises
He gave through His servant Moses.
May the Lord our God be with us as He was with our ancestors;
may He never leave us or abandon us.
May He give us the desire to do His will in everything
and to obey all the commands, decrees, and
regulations that He gave our ancestors.
And may these words that I have prayed
in the presence of the Lord be before Him constantly,
day and night, so that the Lord our God may give justice to me and to
His people...
according to each day's needs. Then people all over the earth
will know
that the Lord alone is God and there is no other.
— *1 Kings 8:56-60*

And now, dear brothers and sisters, we want you to know
what will happen to the believers who have died
so you will not grieve like people who have no hope.

Then, together with them, we who are still alive and remain
on the earth will be caught up [raptured] in the clouds
to meet the Lord in the air. Then we will be with the Lord forever.
— *1 Thessalonians 4:13,17*

Yet what we suffer now is nothing
compared to the glory He will reveal to us later.
— *Romans 8:18*

You will show me the way of life,
granting me the joy of Your presence
and the pleasures of living with You forever.
— *Psalm 16:11*

Create in me a clean heart, O God.
Renew a loyal spirit within me.
— *Psalm 51:10*

Yet I still belong to You;
You hold my right hand.
You guide me with Your counsel,
leading me to a glorious destiny.
— *Psalm 73:23-24*

Then I heard again what sounded like the shout of a vast crowd
or the roar of mighty ocean waves or the crash of loud thunder:
"Praise the Lord!
For the Lord our God, the Almighty, reigns.
Let us be glad and rejoice,
and let us give honor to Him.
For the time has come for the wedding feast of the Lamb,
and His bride has prepared herself.
She has been given the finest of pure white linen to wear."
For the fine linen represents the good deeds of God's holy people.
And the angel said to me, "Write this: Blessed are those who
are invited to the wedding feast of the Lamb."
And he added, "These are true words that come from God."
— *Revelation 19:6-9*

You will keep in perfect peace
all who trust in You,
all whose thoughts are fixed on You!
— *Isaiah 26:3*

Have you never heard?
Have you never understood?
The Lord is the Everlasting God,
the Creator of all the earth.
He never grows weak or weary.
No one can measure the depths of His understanding.
He gives power to the weak
and strength to the powerless.
Even youths will become weak and tired,
and young men will fall in exhaustion.
But those who trust in the Lord will find new strength.
They will soar high on wings like eagles.
They will run and not grow weary.
They will walk and not faint.
— *Isaiah 40:28-31*

Praise the Lord!
For He has heard my cry for mercy.
The Lord is my strength and shield.
I trust Him with all my heart.
He helps me, and my heart is filled with joy.
I burst out in songs of thanksgiving.
The Lord gives His people strength.
He is a safe fortress for His anointed king.
Save Your people!
Bless Israel, Your special possession.
Lead them like a shepherd,
and carry them in Your arms forever.
— *Psalm 28:6-9*

But let me reveal to you a wonderful secret.
We will not all die,
but we will all be transformed!
It will happen in a moment, in the blink of an eye,
when the last trumpet is blown. For when the trumpet sounds,
those who have died will be raised to live forever.
And we who are living will also be transformed.
For our dying bodies must be transformed into bodies that will never die;
our mortal bodies must be transformed into immortal bodies.
Then, when our dying bodies have been transformed
into bodies that will never die,
this Scripture will be fulfilled:
"Death is swallowed up in victory.
O death, where is your victory?
O death, where is your sting?"
For sin is the sting that results in death,
and the law gives sin its power.
But thank God! He gives us victory over sin and death
through our Lord Jesus Christ.
— *1 Corinthians 15:51-57*

But when the Father sends the Advocate as My representative —
that is, the Holy Spirit — He will teach you everything
and will remind you of everything I have told you.
"I am leaving you with a gift — peace of mind and heart.
And the peace I give is a gift the world cannot give.
So don't be troubled or afraid."
— *John 14:26,27*

"For I know the plans I have for you," says the Lord.
"They are plans for good and not for disaster,
to give you a future and a hope.
In those days when you pray, I will listen.
If you look for Me wholeheartedly, you will find Me.
I will be found by you," says the Lord.
"I will end your captivity and restore your fortunes.
I will gather you out of the nations where I sent you
and will bring you home again to your own land."
— *Jeremiah 29:11-14*

But now, as to whether the dead will be raised —
haven't you ever read about this in the writings of Moses,
in the story of the burning bush? Long after Abraham,
Isaac, and Jacob had died, God said to Moses, 'I am the God of Abraham,
the God of Isaac, and the God of Jacob.'
So He is the God of the living, not the dead.
You have made a serious error.
— *Mark 12:26-27*

Don't be afraid, for I am with you.
Don't be discouraged, for I am your God.
I will strengthen you and help you.
I will hold you up with My victorious right hand.

For I hold you by your right hand—
I, the Lord your God.
And I say to you,
'Don't be afraid. I am here to help you.'
— *Isaiah 41:10,13*

Rejoice the soul of Your servant,
for unto You do I lift up my soul.
— *Psalm 86:4 NKJV*

Then you will experience God's peace,
which exceeds anything we can understand.
His peace will guard your hearts and minds as you live in Christ Jesus.
And now, dear brothers and sisters, one final thing.
Fix your thoughts on what is true, and honorable,
and right, and pure, and lovely, and admirable.
Think about things that are excellent and worthy of praise.
Keep putting into practice all you learned and received from Me —
everything you heard from Me and saw Me doing.
Then the God of peace will be with you.
— *Philippians 4:7-9*

And God will generously provide all you need.
Then you will always have everything you need
and plenty left over to share with others.
— *2 Corinthians 9:8*

Now all glory to God, Who is able, through His mighty power
at work within us, to accomplish infinitely more than we might ask or think.
— *Ephesians 3:20*

Now all glory to God, Who is able to keep you from falling away
and will bring you with great joy
into His glorious presence without a single fault.
— *Jude 24*

David begged God to spare the child.

He went without food and lay all night on the bare ground.

The elders of his household pleaded with him to get up

and eat with them, but he refused.

Then on the seventh day the child died.

David's advisers were afraid to tell him. "He wouldn't listen to reason

while the child was ill," they said.

"What drastic thing will he do when we tell him the child is dead?"

When David saw them whispering, he realized what had happened.

"Is the child dead?"

he asked. "Yes," they replied, "he is dead."

Then David got up from the ground, washed himself,

put on lotions, and changed his clothes.

He went to the Tabernacle and worshiped the Lord.

After that, he returned to the palace and was served food and ate.

His advisers were amazed. "We don't understand you," they told him.

"While the child was still living, you wept and refused to eat.

But now that the child is dead, you have stopped your

mourning and are eating again."

David replied, "I fasted and wept while the child was alive, for I said,

'Perhaps the Lord will be gracious to me and let the child live.'

But why should I fast when he is dead?

Can I bring him back again? I will go to him one day,

but he cannot return to me."

— 2 Samuel 12:16-23

May God our Father and the Lord Jesus Christ give you grace and peace.

All praise to God, the Father of our Lord Jesus Christ.

God is our merciful Father and the source of all comfort.

He comforts us in all our troubles so that we can comfort others.

When they are troubled, we will be able to

give them the same comfort God has given us.

For the more we suffer for Christ,

the more God will shower us with his comfort through Christ.

Even when we are weighed down with troubles, it is for

your comfort and salvation!

For when we ourselves are comforted, we will certainly comfort you.

Then you can patiently endure the same things we suffer.

We are confident that as you share in our sufferings,

you will also share in the comfort God gives us.

We think you ought to know, dear brothers and sisters,

about the trouble we went through...

We were crushed and overwhelmed beyond our ability to endure,

and we thought we would never live through it.

In fact, we expected to die. But as a result, we stopped relying on ourselves

and learned to rely only on God, Who raises the dead.

And He did rescue us from mortal danger, and He will rescue us again.

We have placed our confidence in Him, and He will continue to rescue us.

And you are helping us by praying for us. Then many

people will give thanks

because God has graciously answered so many prayers for our safety.

— *2 Corinthians 1:2-10*

Therefore He is able, once and forever, to save those
who come to God through Him. He lives forever to
intercede with God on their behalf.
— *Hebrews 7:25*

Then I heard a loud voice shouting across the heavens,
"It has come at last — salvation and power
and the Kingdom of our God,
and the authority of His Christ.
For the accuser of our brothers and sisters
has been thrown down to earth —
the one who accuses them
before our God day and night.
And they have defeated Him by the Blood of the Lamb
and by their testimony [of all the Blood does]
And they did not love their lives so much
that they were afraid to die."
— *Revelation 12:10-11*

Give your burdens to the Lord,
and He will take care of you.
He will not permit the godly to slip and fall.
— *Psalm 55:22*

The way of the righteous is like the first gleam of dawn,
which shines ever brighter until the [perfect] full light of day.
— *Proverbs 4:18*

But the other criminal protested, "Don't you fear God
even when you have been sentenced to die?
We deserve to die for our crimes, but this Man hasn't done anything wrong."
Then he said, "Jesus, remember me when You come into Your Kingdom."
And Jesus replied, "I assure you, today you will be with Me in paradise."
— *Luke 23:40-43*

Give all your worries and cares to God, for He cares about you.
— *1 Peter 5:7*

Then the angel showed me Jeshua the high priest standing before the angel of the Lord.

The Accuser, Satan, was there at the angel's right hand, making accusations against Jeshua.

And the Lord said to Satan, "I, the Lord, reject your accusations, Satan.

Yes, the Lord... rebukes you.

This man is like a burning stick that has been snatched from the fire."

Jeshua's clothing was filthy [rags] as he stood there before the angel.

So the angel said to the others standing there, "Take off his filthy [rags],"

And turning to Jeshua he said, "See, I have taken away your sins,

and now I am giving you these fine new [clean] clothes."

Then I said, "They should also place a clean turban on his head."

So they put a clean priestly turban on his head and dressed him in new clothes...

Then the angel of the Lord spoke very solemnly to Jeshua and said,

"This is what the Lord of Heaven's Armies says: If you follow My ways

and carefully serve Me, then you will be given

authority over My Temple and its courtyards.

I will let you walk among these others standing here."

— *Zechariah 3:1-7*

For everyone has sinned; we all fall short of God's glorious standard.

— *Romans 3:23*

It's your sins that have cut you off from God.
Because of your sins, He has turned away
and will not listen anymore.
— Isaiah 59:2

If you look for Me wholeheartedly, you will find Me.
— Jeremiah 29:13

I love all who love Me.
Those who search will surely find Me.

For whoever finds Me finds life
and receives favor from the Lord.
— Proverbs 8:17,35

Keep on asking, and you will receive what you ask for.
Keep on seeking, and you will find.
Keep on knocking, and the door will be opened to you.
For everyone who asks, receives.
Everyone who seeks, finds.
And to everyone who knocks, the door will be opened.
— *Matthew 7:7-8*

This means that anyone who belongs to Christ
has become a new person.
The old life is gone; a new life has begun!

For God made Christ, who never sinned,
to be [sin] and the offering for our sin,
so that we could be made right with God through Christ.
— *2 Corinthians 5:17,21*

Faith shows the reality of what we hope for;
it is the evidence of things we cannot see.
And it is impossible to please God without faith.
Anyone who wants to come to Him must believe that God exists
and that He rewards those who sincerely seek Him.
— *Hebrews 11:1,6*

But God showed His great love for us
by sending Christ to die for us while we were still sinners.
And since we have been made right in God's sight by the blood of Christ,
He will certainly save us from God's condemnation.
For since our friendship with God was restored by the death of His Son
while we were still His enemies,
we will certainly be saved through the life of His Son.
— *Romans 5:8-10*

Ask Me and I will tell you remarkable secrets
you do not know about things to come.
— *Jeremiah 33:3*

And you know that Jesus came to take away our sins,
and there is no sin in Him.

But when people keep on sinning, it shows that they belong to the devil,
who has been sinning since the beginning.
But the Son of God came to destroy the works of the devil.

Even if we feel guilty,
God is greater than our feelings, and He knows everything.
— *1 John 3:5,8,20*

Repent therefore and be converted,
that your sins may be blotted out,
so that times of refreshing may come from the presence of the Lord,
— *Acts 3:19 NKJV*

And don't say, 'Who will go down to the place of the dead?'
(to bring Christ back to life again).

If you openly declare that Jesus is Lord
and believe in your heart that God raised Him from the dead,
you will be saved.

For it is by believing in your heart that you are made right with God,
and it is by openly declaring your faith that you are saved.
— *Romans 10:7,9,10*

Don't let your hearts be troubled. Trust in God, and trust also in Me.

Jesus told him, "I am the way, the truth, and the life.
No one can come to the Father except through Me."
— *John 14:1,6*

You say, 'I am rich. I have everything I want. I don't need a thing!'
And you don't realize that you are wretched and miserable
and poor and blind and naked. So I advise you to buy gold from Me —
gold that has been purified by fire. Then you will be rich.
Also buy white garments from Me so you will not be shamed by your nakedness,
and ointment for your eyes so you will be able to see.
I correct and discipline everyone I love.
So be diligent and turn from your indifference.
"Look! I stand at the door and knock. If you hear My voice and open the door,
I will come in, and we will share a meal together as friends.
Those who are victorious will sit with Me on My throne,
just as I was victorious and sat with My Father on His throne."
— *Revelations 3:17-21*

Notes:

SECTION 11

Everything You've Wanted to Know About Heaven

Yet God has made everything beautiful for its own time.
He has planted eternity in the human heart,
but even so, people cannot see the whole scope of God's work from
beginning to end.

— Ecclesiastes 3:11

Don't let your hearts be troubled. Trust in God, and trust also in Me.
There is more than enough room in My Father's home. If this were not so,
would I have told you that I am going to prepare a place for you?
When everything is ready, I will come and get you,
so that you will always be with Me
where I am. And you know the way to where I am going.

— John 14:1-4

Father, I want these whom You have given Me to be with Me where I am.
Then they can see all the glory You gave Me because You loved Me
even before the world began!

— John 17:24

May you hear the humble and earnest requests from me and Your people...
when we pray toward this place. Yes, hear us from heaven
where You live, and when You hear, forgive.
— *1 Kings 8:30*

But we are citizens of heaven, where the Lord Jesus Christ lives.
And we are eagerly waiting for Him to return as our Savior.
— *Philippians 3:20*

But they were looking for a better place, a heavenly homeland.
That is why God is not ashamed to be called their God,
for He has prepared a city for them.
— *Hebrews 11:16*

**The Lord has made the heavens His throne;
from there He rules over everything.**
— *Psalm 103:19*

**I was caught up to the third heaven fourteen years ago.
Whether I was in my body or out of my body, I don't know—only God knows.
Yes, only God knows whether I was in my body or outside my body.
But I do know that I was caught up to paradise and heard things so astounding
that they cannot be expressed in words, things no human is allowed to tell.**
— *2 Corinthians 12:2-4*

**In the same way, let your good deeds shine out for all to see,
so that everyone will praise your heavenly Father.**
— *Matthew 5:16*

That is what the Scriptures mean when they say,
"No eye has seen, no ear has heard,
and no mind has imagined
what God has prepared
for those who love Him."
But it was to us that God revealed these things by His Spirit.
For His Spirit searches out everything
and shows us God's deep secrets.
— *1 Corinthians 2:9-10*

Pray like this:
Our Father in heaven,
may Your name be kept holy.
— *Matthew 6:9*

As they strained to see Him rising into heaven,
two white-robed men suddenly stood among them. "Men of Galilee," they said,
"why are you standing here staring into heaven?
Jesus has been taken from you into heaven,
but someday He will return from heaven
in the same way you saw Him go!"
— *Acts 1:10-11*

For He raised us from the dead along with Christ
and seated us with Him in the heavenly realms
because we are united with Christ Jesus.
— *Ephesians 2:6*

And Jesus replied, "I assure you,
today you will be with Me in paradise."
— *Luke 23:43*

For the Son of Man will come with His angels
in the glory of His Father and will judge all people
according to their deeds.
— *Matthew 16:27*

And Jesus replied, "I assure you, today you will be with Me in paradise."
— Luke 23:43

Then the angel showed me a river with the water of life, clear as crystal,

flowing from the throne of God and of the Lamb.

It flowed down the center of the main street. On each side of the river

grew a tree of life, bearing twelve crops of fruit, with a fresh crop each month.

The leaves were used for medicine to heal the nations.

No longer will there be a curse upon anything. For the throne of God and of the Lamb

will be there, and His servants will worship Him. And they will see His face,

and His name will be written on their foreheads. And there will be no night there —

no need for lamps or sun — for the Lord God will shine on them.

And they will reign forever and ever.

— Revelation 22:1-5

When Jesus had tasted it, He said, "It is finished!"
Then He bowed His head and gave up His spirit.
— John 19:30

But if we are living in the light, as God is in the light,
then we have fellowship with each other, and the blood of Jesus, His Son,
cleanses us from all sin.
— *1 John 1:7*

So now there is no condemnation for those who belong to Christ Jesus.
— *Romans 8:1*

Yet now He has reconciled you to Himself through the death of Christ
in His physical body. As a result, He has brought you into His own presence,
and you are holy and blameless as you stand before Him without a single fault.
— *Colossians 1:22*

Now all glory to God, who is able to keep you from falling away
and will bring you with great joy into His glorious Presence without a single fault.
— *Jude 1:24*

Yes, we are fully confident, and we would rather be
away from these earthly bodies,
for then we will be at Home with the Lord.
— *2 Corinthians 5:8*

You have already been [cleansed], pruned and purified
by the [Word] I have given you.
— *John 15:3*

So God can point to us in all future ages as examples
of the incredible wealth of His grace and kindness toward us,
as shown in all He has done for us who are united with Christ Jesus.
— *Ephesians 2:7*

Since you have been raised to new life with Christ,
set your sights [affections] on the realities of heaven,
where Christ sits in the place of honor at God's right hand.
Think about the things of heaven, not the things of earth.
For you died to this life, and your real life is hidden with Christ in God.
— *Colossians 3:1-3*

Father, I want these whom You have given Me
to be with Me where I am. Then they can see all the glory You gave Me
because You loved Me even before the world began!
— *John 17:24*

You have come to the assembly of God's firstborn children,
whose names are written in heaven. You have come to God Himself,
Who is the Judge over all things.
You have come to the spirits of the righteous ones in heaven
who have now been made perfect.

—- *Hebrews 12:23*

Then I saw a new heaven and a new earth, for the old heaven and the old earth
had disappeared. And the sea was also gone. And I saw the holy city,
the New Jerusalem, coming down from God out of heaven like a bride
beautifully dressed for her Husband.
I heard a loud shout from the throne, saying, "Look,
God's home is now among His people! He will live with them,
and they will be His people. God Himself will be with them.
He will wipe every tear from their eyes, and there will be no more death
or sorrow or crying or pain. All these things are gone forever."
And the One sitting on the throne said, "Look, I am making everything new!"
And then He said to me, "Write this down, for what I tell you
is trustworthy and true."

— *Revelations 21:1-5*

Store up your treasures in heaven,
where moths and rust cannot destroy,
and thieves do not break in and steal.

— *Matthew 6:20*

And we have a priceless inheritance —
an inheritance that is kept in heaven for you,
pure and undefiled, beyond the reach of change and decay.
— *1 Peter 1:4*

He thought it was better to suffer for the sake of Christ
than to own the treasures of Egypt,
for he was looking ahead to his great reward.
— *Hebrews 11:26*

You will show me the way of life,
granting me the joy of Your presence
and the pleasures of living with You forever.
— *Psalm 16:11*

For we must all stand before Christ to be judged.
We will each receive whatever we deserve for
the good or evil we have done in this earthly body.
— *2 Corinthians 5:10*

After he was crowned king, he returned and called in the servants
to whom he had given the money. He wanted to find out
what their profits were. The first servant reported,
'Master, I invested your money and made ten times the original amount!'
'Well done!' the king exclaimed. 'You are a good [and faithful] servant.
You have been faithful with the little I entrusted to you,
so you will be governor [ruler] of ten cities as your reward.'
The next servant reported, 'Master, I invested your money
and made five times the original amount.'
'Well done!' the king said. 'You will be governor [ruler] over five cities.'
— *Luke 19:15-19*

So why do you condemn another believer?
Why do you look down on another believer?
Remember, we will all stand before the judgment seat of God.
— *Romans 14:10*

The servant to whom he had entrusted the five bags of silver came forward
with five more and said, 'Master, you gave me five bags of silver to invest,
and I have earned five more.'
The master was full of praise. 'Well done, my good and faithful servant!
You have been faithful in handling this small amount,
so now I will give you many more responsibilities.'
Let's celebrate together!'
— *Matthew 25:20-21*

For no one can lay any foundation other than the one we already have —
Jesus Christ. Anyone who builds on that foundation may use a variety of materials —
gold, silver, jewels, wood, hay, or straw. But on the judgment day, fire will reveal
what kind of work each builder has done. The fire will show
if a person's work has any value. If the work survives,
that builder will receive a reward. But if the work is burned up,
the builder will suffer great loss. The builder will be saved,
but like someone barely escaping through a wall of flames.
— *1 Corinthians 3:11-15*

After all, what gives us hope and joy, and what will be our proud reward and crown as we stand before our Lord Jesus when He returns? It is you!
— *1 Thessalonians 2:19*

Don't you realize that in a race everyone runs,
but only one person gets the prize? So run to win!
All athletes are disciplined in their training. They do it to win a prize
that will fade away, but we do it for an eternal prize.
So I run with purpose in every step. I am not just shadowboxing.
I discipline my body like an athlete, training it to do what it should.
Otherwise, I fear that after preaching to others I myself might be
disqualified.
— *1 Corinthians 9:24-27*

And now the prize awaits me — the crown of righteousness, which the Lord, the righteous Judge, will give me on the day of His return. And the prize is not just for me but for all who eagerly look forward to His appearing.
— *2 Timothy 4:8*

So prepare your minds for action and exercise self-control.
Put all your hope in the gracious salvation that will come to you
when Jesus Christ is revealed to the world.
— *1 Peter 1:13*

Don't be afraid of what you are about to suffer.
The devil will throw some of you into prison to test you.
You will suffer for ten days.
But if you remain faithful even when facing death,
I will give you the crown of life.
— *Revelations 2:10*

And when the Great Shepherd appears, you will receive a crown
of never-ending glory and honor.
— *1 Peter 5:4*

My child, if your heart is wise,
My own heart will rejoice [even Mine!]
— *Proverbs 23:15*

The twenty-four elders fall down and worship the One
sitting on the throne
(the One Who lives forever and ever). And they lay their crowns
before the throne
and say, "You are worthy, O Lord our God,
to receive glory and honor and power.
For You created all things,
and they exist because You created [them for Your pleasure]."
— *Revelations 4:10-11*

For you said to yourself,
'I will ascend to heaven and set my throne above God's stars.
I will preside on the mountain of the gods
far away in the north.'
— *Isaiah 14:13*

Now we see things imperfectly, like puzzling reflections in a mirror,
but then we will see everything with perfect clarity. All that I know now
is partial and incomplete, but then I will know everything completely,
just as God now knows me completely.

— 1 Corinthians 13:12

The master was full of praise. 'Well done, my good and faithful servant.
You have been faithful in handling this small amount,
so now I will give you many more responsibilities.
Let's celebrate together!'

— Matthew 25:21

And from Jesus Christ. He is the faithful witness to these things,
the first to rise from the dead, and the Ruler of all the kings of the world.
All glory to Him Who loves us and has freed us from our sins
by shedding His blood for us. He has made us a Kingdom of priests
for God His Father. All glory and power to Him forever and ever! Amen.

— Revelations 1:5-6

Jesus went on to say, "I tell you the truth, some standing here right now

will not die before they see the Kingdom of God arrive in great power!"

Six days later Jesus took Peter, James, and John, and led them up a high mountain

to be alone. As the men watched, Jesus' appearance was transformed,

and His clothes became dazzling white, far whiter than any earthly bleach

could ever make them. Then Elijah and Moses appeared and began talking with Jesus.

Peter exclaimed, "Rabbi, it's wonderful for us to be here!

Let's make three shelters as memorials — one for You, one for Moses,

and one for Elijah." He said this because he didn't really know what else to say,

for they were all terrified. Then a cloud overshadowed them, and a voice from the cloud

said, "This is My dearly loved Son. Listen to Him." Suddenly, when they looked around,

Moses and Elijah were gone, and they saw only Jesus with them.

As they went back down the mountain, He told them not to tell anyone

what they had seen until the Son of Man had risen from the dead.

So they kept it to themselves, but they often asked each other

what He meant by "rising from the dead."

— Mark 9:1-10

Jesus said, "There was a certain rich man who was splendidly clothed in purple and fine linen and who lived each day in luxury. At his gate lay a poor man named Lazarus who was covered with sores. As Lazarus lay there longing for scraps from the rich man's table, the dogs would come and lick his open sores. "Finally, the poor man died and was carried by the angels to sit beside Abraham at the heavenly banquet. The rich man also died and was buried, and he went to the place of the dead. There, in torment, he saw Abraham in the far distance with Lazarus at his side. The rich man shouted, 'Father Abraham, have some pity! Send Lazarus over here to dip the tip of his finger in water and cool my tongue. I am in anguish in these flames.' But Abraham said to him, 'Son, remember that during your lifetime you had everything you wanted, and Lazarus had nothing. So now he is here being comforted, and you are in anguish. And besides, there is a great chasm separating us. No one can cross over to you from Here, and no one can cross over to us from there.' Then the rich man said, 'Please, Father Abraham, at least send him to my father's home. For I have five brothers, and I want him to warn them so they don't end up in this place of torment.' But Abraham said, 'Moses and the prophets have warned them. Your brothers can read what they wrote.' The rich man replied, 'No, Father Abraham! But if someone is sent to them from the dead, then they will repent of their sins and turn to God.' But Abraham said, 'If they won't listen to Moses and the prophets, they won't be persuaded even if someone rises from the dead.'"

— *Luke 16:19-31*

And they sang a new song with these words:
"You are worthy to take the scroll
and break its seals and open it.
For You were slaughtered, and Your blood has
ransomed people for God
from every tribe and language and people and nation.
And You have caused them to become
a [kings and priests] for our God.
And they will reign on the earth."
— *Revelations 5:9-10*

Then I saw thrones, and the people sitting on them had been given the authority
to judge. And I saw the souls of those who had been beheaded for their testimony
about Jesus and for proclaiming the Word of God. They had not worshiped the beast
or his statue, nor accepted his mark on their foreheads or their hands.
They all came to life again, and they reigned with Christ for a thousand years.
This is the first resurrection. (The rest of the dead did not come back to life
until the thousand years had ended.) Blessed and holy are those who
share in the first resurrection. For them the second death
holds no power, but they will be priests of God
and of Christ and will reign with Him a thousand years.
— *Revelations 20:4-6*

SECTION 12

*How Can You Be Sure You'll Be
With Them in Heaven?*

"You can enter God's Kingdom only through the narrow gate.
The highway to hell is broad, and its gate is wide for the many who
choose that way.
But the gateway to Life is very narrow and the road is difficult, and
only a few ever find it."
— *Matthew 7:13-14*

But you are to be perfect, even as your Father in heaven is perfect.
— *Matthew 5:48*

Trust in the Lord with all your heart;
do not depend on your own [self's] understanding.
Seek His will in all you do,
and He will show you which path to take.

For the Lord is your security.
He will keep your foot from being caught in a trap.
— *Proverbs 3:5-6,26*

But now you must be holy in everything you do,
just as God Who chose you is holy.
For the Scriptures say, "You must be holy because I am holy."
— *1 Peter 1:15-16*

We are human, but we don't wage war as humans do.
We use God's mighty weapons, not worldly weapons,
to knock down the strongholds of human [feelings and] reasoning
and to destroy false [imaginations and] arguments.
We destroy every proud obstacle that keeps people from knowing God.
We capture [our and] their rebellious thoughts
and [force and] teach them to obey Christ.

Look at the obvious facts [don't just judge by the outward appearance].
Those who say they belong to Christ must recognize that
we belong to Christ as much as they do.
— *2 Corinthians 10:3-5,7*

So whether you eat or drink, or whatever you do,
do it all for the glory of God.
— *1 Corinthians 10:31*

SECTION 13

Powerful Resources for Your Daily Dose of Peace

Have mercy upon me, O God,

According to Your lovingkindness;

According to the multitude of Your tender mercies,

Blot out my transgressions.

Wash me thoroughly from my iniquity,

And cleanse me from my sin.

For I acknowledge my transgressions,

And my sin is always before me.

Against You, You only, have I sinned,

And done this evil in Your sight—

That You may be found just when You speak,

And blameless when You judge.

Behold, I was brought forth in iniquity,

And in sin my mother conceived me.

Behold, You desire truth in the inward parts,

And in the hidden part You will make me to know wisdom.

Purge me with hyssop, and I shall be clean;

Wash me, and I shall be whiter than snow.

Make me hear joy and gladness,

That the bones You have broken may rejoice.

Hide Your face from my sins,

And blot out all my iniquities.

Create in me a clean heart [all You desire in me], O God,

And renew a steadfast [pleasing to You] spirit within me.

— *Psalm 51:1-10 NKJV*

This is the message we heard from Jesus and now declare to you:
God is light, and there is no darkness in Him at all.
So we are lying if we say we have fellowship with God
but go on living in spiritual darkness;
we are not practicing the truth. But if we are living in the light,
as God is in the light, then we have fellowship with each other,
and the Blood of Jesus, His Son, cleanses us from all sin.
If we claim we have no sin, we are only fooling ourselves
and not living in the truth. But if we confess our sins to Him,
He is faithful and just to forgive us our sins and to cleanse us
from all wickedness.
— 1 John 1:5-9

For God made Christ, who never sinned,
to be [sin and] the offering for our sin,
so that we could be made right with God through Christ.
— 2 Corinthians 5:21

He does not punish us for all our sins;
He does not deal harshly with us, as we deserve.
For His unfailing love toward those who fear Him
is as great as the height of the heavens above the earth.
He has removed our sins as far from us
as the east is from the west.
The Lord is like a father to His children,
tender and compassionate to those who fear Him.
For He knows how weak we are;
He remembers we are only dust.
— Psalm 103:10-14

Rejoice the soul of Your servant,

For to You, O Lord, I lift up my soul.

For You, Lord, are good, and ready to forgive,

And abundant in mercy to all those who call upon You.

Give ear, O Lord, to my prayer;

And attend to the voice of my supplications.

In the day of my trouble I will call upon You,

For You will answer me.

Among the gods there is none like You, O Lord;

Nor are there any works like Your works.

All nations whom You have made

Shall come and worship before You, O Lord,

And shall glorify Your name.

For You are great, and do wondrous things;

You alone are God.

Teach me Your way, O Lord;

I will walk in Your truth;

Unite my heart to fear Your name.

I will praise You, O Lord my God, with all my heart,

And I will glorify Your name forevermore.

For great is Your mercy toward me,

And You have delivered my soul from the depths of hell;

O God, the proud have risen against me,

And a mob of violent men have sought my life,

And have not set You before them.

But You, O Lord, are a God full of compassion, and gracious,

longsuffering and abundant in mercy and truth.

Oh, turn to me, and have mercy on me!

Give Your strength to Your servant,

And save the son of Your maidservant.

Show me a sign for good,

That those who hate me may see it and be ashamed,

Because You, Lord, have helped me and comforted me.

— *Psalm 86:4-17 NKJV*

To illustrate the point further, Jesus told them this story:
"A man had two sons. The younger son told his father, 'I want my share of your estate
now before you die.' So his father agreed to divide his wealth between his sons.
A few days later this younger son packed all his belongings and moved to a distant
land, and there he wasted all his money in wild living. About the time his money ran
out, a great famine swept over the land, and he began to starve. He persuaded a local
farmer to hire him, and the man sent him into his fields to feed the pigs. The young
man became so hungry that even the pods he was feeding the pigs looked good to
him. But no one gave him anything.
When he finally came to his senses, he said to himself, 'At home even the hired
servants have food enough to spare, and here I am dying of hunger! I will go home to
my father and say, 'Father, I have sinned against both heaven and you,
and I am no longer worthy
of being called your son. Please take me on as a hired servant.'
So he returned home to his father. And while he was still a long way off,
his father saw him coming. Filled with love and compassion,
he ran to his son, embraced him, and kissed him.
His son said to him, 'Father, I have sinned against both heaven and you, and I am no
longer worthy of being called your son.' But his father said to the servants, 'Quick!
Bring the finest robe in the house and put it on him.
Get a ring for his finger and sandals for his feet."

— *Luke 15:11-22*

Don't be concerned for your own good but for the good of others.
So whether you eat or drink, or whatever you do,
do it all for the glory of God.
— *1 Corinthians 10:24,31*

'And you must love the Lord your God
with all your heart, all your soul, all your mind,
and all your strength.' The second is equally important:
'Love your neighbor as yourself.'
No other commandment is greater than these.
— *Mark 12:30-31*

You were cleansed from your sins when you obeyed the truth,
so now you must show sincere love to each other
as brothers and sisters. Love each other deeply with all your heart.
— *1 Peter 1:22*

Either way, Christ's love controls us. Since we believe that Christ died for all,
we also believe that we have all died to our old life.
He died for everyone so that those who receive His new life
will no longer live for themselves.
Instead, they will live for Christ, Who died and was raised for them.
So we have stopped evaluating others from a human point of view.
At one time we thought of Christ merely from a human point of view.
How differently we know Him now!
This means that anyone who belongs to Christ has become a new person.
The old life is gone; a new life [in the Spirit] has begun!
— 2 Corinthians 5:14-17

Yet I still dare to hope
when I remember this:
The faithful love of the Lord never ends!
His mercies never cease.
Great is His faithfulness;
His mercies begin afresh each morning.
I say to myself, "The Lord is my inheritance;
therefore, I will hope in Him!"
The Lord is good to those who depend on Him,
to those who search for Him.
So it is good to wait quietly
— Lamentations 3:21-26

Therefore if there is any consolation in Christ,

if any comfort of love, if any fellowship of the Spirit,

if any affection and mercy, fulfill My joy by being like-minded,

having the same love, being of one accord, of one mind.

Let nothing be done through selfish ambition or conceit,

but in lowliness of mind let each esteem others better than himself.

Let each of you look out not only for his own interests,

but also for the interests of others.

Let this mind be in you which was also in Christ Jesus,

Who, being in the form of God, did not consider it robbery to be equal with God,

but made Himself of no reputation, taking the form of a bondservant,

and coming in the likeness of men. And being found in appearance as a man,

He humbled Himself and became obedient to the point of death,

even the death of the Cross. Therefore God also has highly exalted Him

and given Him the name which is above every name,

that at the name of Jesus every knee should bow,

of those in heaven, and of those on earth, and of those under the earth,

and that every tongue should confess that Jesus Christ is Lord,

to the glory of God the Father.

Therefore, my beloved, as you have always obeyed,

not as in my presence only, but now much more in my absence,

work out your own salvation with fear and trembling;

for it is God who works in you

both to will and to do for His good pleasure.

— *Philippians 2:1-13*

(read 2:13 & 4:13 in the AMPC version)

Notes:

SECTION 14

Home at Last! Free at Last!

A good reputation is more valuable than costly perfume.
And the day you die is better than the day you are born.
Finishing is better than starting.
Patience is better than pride.

— *Ecclesiastes 7:1,8*

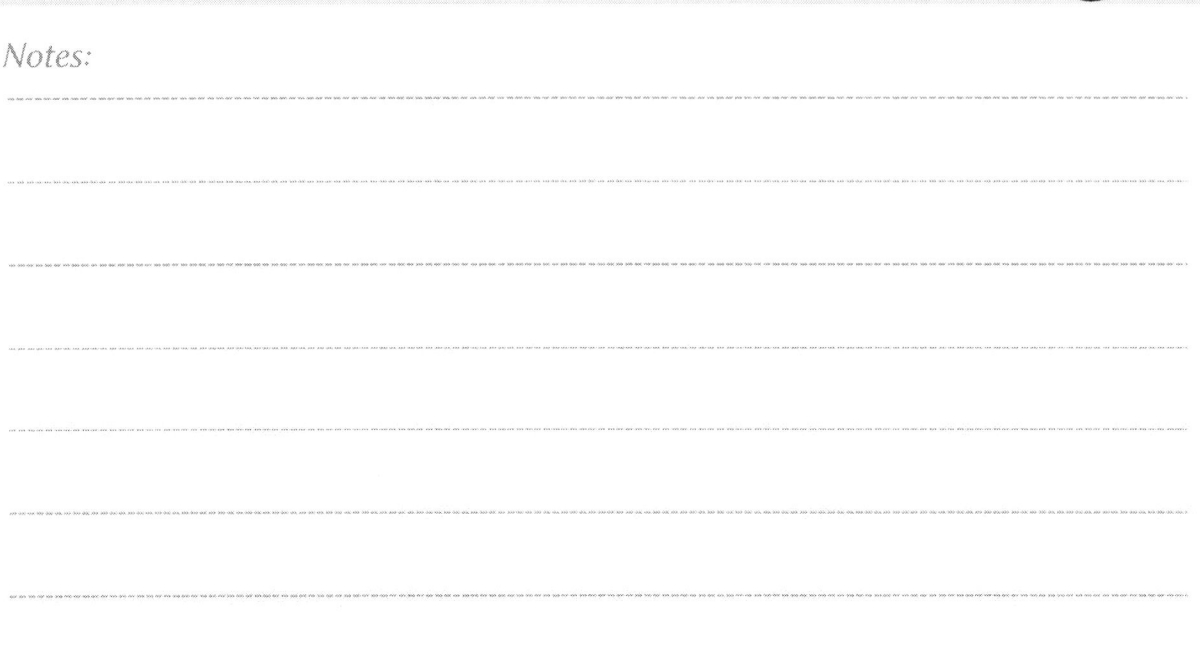

You will show me the way of life,
granting me the joy of Your presence
and the pleasures of living with You forever.

— *Psalm 16:11*

Notes:

_____

_____

_____

_____

_____

_____

SECTION 15

How to Get Victory
Over Your Negative Feelings

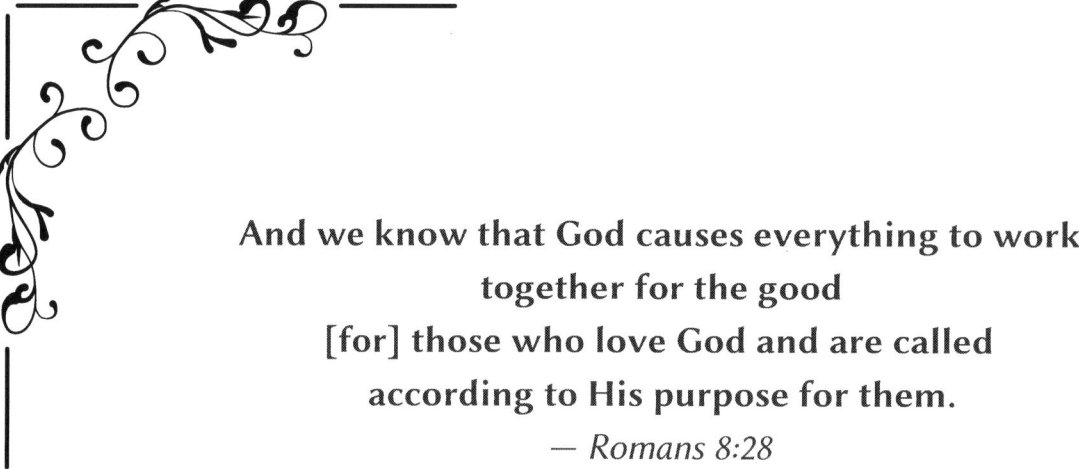

And we know that God causes everything to work
together for the good
[for] those who love God and are called
according to His purpose for them.
— *Romans 8:28*

The Lord will work out His plans for my life —
for Your faithful love, O Lord, endures forever.
Don't abandon me, for You made me.
— *Psalm 138:8*

I cry out to God Most High,
to God Who will fulfill His purpose for me.
— *Psalm 57:2*

From six disasters He will rescue you;
even in the seventh, He will keep you from evil.
— *Job 5:19*

But He knows where I am going.
And when He tests me, I will come out as pure as gold.
For I have stayed on God's paths;
I have followed His ways and not turned aside.
I have not departed from His commands,
but have treasured His words more than daily food.
But once He has made His decision, who can change His mind?
Whatever He wants to do, He does.
So He will do to me whatever He has planned.
He controls my destiny.
— *Job 23:10-14*

SECTION 16

The Two Major Grief Choices Available to You:

Backward Grief vs. Forward Grief

Don't let your hearts be troubled. Trust in God, and trust also in Me.
There is more than enough room in My Father's home.
If this were not so, would I have told you that I am going to prepare a
place for you?
When everything is ready, I will come and get you,
so that you will always be with me where I am.
— *John 14:1-3*

While we look forward with hope to that wonderful day
when the glory of our Great God and Savior, Jesus Christ,
will be revealed.
— *Titus 2:13*

No, dear brothers and sisters, I have not achieved [perfection],
but I focus on this one thing: Forgetting the past
and looking forward to what lies ahead,
I press on to reach the end of the race
and receive the heavenly prize for which God, through Christ Jesus,
is calling us.
— *Philippians 3:13-14*

"But forget all that— it is nothing compared to what I am going to do. For I am about to do something new. See, I have already begun! Do you not see it? I will make a pathway through the wilderness. I will create rivers in the dry wasteland.
— *Isiah 43:18-19*

Remember what happened to Lot's wife! If you cling to your life, you will lose it, and if you let your life go, you will save it.
— *Luke 17:32*

Since you have been raised to new life with Christ, set your sights on the realities of heaven, where Christ sits in the place of honor at God's right hand. Think about the things of heaven, not the things of earth. For you died to this life, and your real life is hidden with Christ in God.
— *Colossians 3:1-3*

Since you have been raised to new life with Christ,
set your sights [affections] on the realities of heaven,
where Christ sits in the place of honor at God's right hand.
Think about the things of heaven, not the things of earth.
For [your old self] died to this life, and your real life is hidden
with Christ in God.
And when Christ, who is your life, is revealed to the whole world,
you will share in all His glory.
— *Colossians 3:1-4*

And now, dear brothers and sisters, we want you to know
what will happen to the believers who have died
so you will not grieve like people who have no hope.
For since we believe that Jesus died and was raised to life again,
we also believe that when Jesus returns,
God will bring back with Him the believers who have died.
We tell you this directly from the Lord:
We who are still living when the Lord returns will not meet Him
ahead of those who have died.
For the Lord Himself will come down from heaven with a commanding shout,
with the voice of the archangel, and with the trumpet call of God.
First, the believers who have died will rise from their graves.
Then, together with them, we who are still alive and remain on the earth
will be caught up [raptured] in the clouds to meet the Lord in the air.
Then we will be with the Lord forever.
— *1 Thessalonians 4:13-17*

SECTION 17

The Forward-Grieving Lifestyle

Why are you cast down, O my soul?
and why are you disquieted in me?
hope in God: for I shall yet praise Him
for *the help of His countenance...*
Why are you cast down, O my soul?
and why are you disquieted within me?
hope in God: for I shall yet praise Him,
Who is *the health of my countenance, and my God.*
— *Psalm 42:5,11 KJV*
(look closely at the italics)

Notes:

SECTION 18

Your Mindset-Reset Model Prayer Template

Then call on Me when you are in trouble,
and I will rescue you,
and you will give Me glory."

— *Psalm 50:1*

Notes:

SECTION 19

Strength for Your
Victorious Journey Homeward

For I can do everything through Christ, Who gives me strength.
— Philippians 4:13

**I have strength for all things in Christ Who strengthens me
[I am ready for anything, and equal to anything
through Him Who infuses inner strength into me;
I am self-sufficient in Christ's sufficiency]!**
— Philippians 4:13 AMPC

**For God is working in you,
giving you the desire and the power to do what pleases Him.**
— Philippians 2:13

**[Not in your own strength] for it is God Who is all the while
effectually at work in you [energizing and creating in you the power
and desire], both to will and to work
for His good pleasure and satisfaction and delight.**
— Philippians 2:13 AMPC

Notes:

SECTION 20

Victorious Grief in a Nutshell

**Since you have been raised to new life with Christ,
set your sights [affections] on the realities of heaven,
where Christ sits in the place of honor at God's right hand
Think about the things of heaven, not the things of earth.**

— Colossians 3:1-2

**You will keep in perfect peace
all who trust in You,
all whose thoughts are fixed on You!
Trust in the Lord always,
for the Lord God is the eternal Rock.**

— Isaiah 26:3-4

Notes:

_____

_____

_____

_____

_____

_____

SECTION 21

Victorious Grief Step by Step,
Thought by Thought, Choice by Choice

Trust in the Lord with all your heart;
do not depend on your own [self's] understanding.
Seek His will in all you do,
and He will show you which path to take.
— *Proverbs 3:5-6*

We are human, but we don't wage war as humans do.
We use God's mighty weapons, not worldly weapons,
to knock down the strongholds of human [feelings and] reasoning
and to destroy false [imaginations and] arguments.
We destroy every proud obstacle that keeps people from knowing
[and obeying] God.
We capture [our own and] their rebellious thoughts and teach [and
force] them to obey Christ.
— *2 Corinthians 10:3-5*

You have turned for me my mourning into dancing;
You have put off my sackcloth and clothed me with gladness,
To the end that my glory may sing praise to You and not be silent.
O Lord my God, I will give thanks to You forever.
— *Psalm 30:11-12*

Notes:

Notes:---

Notes:

> Peace I leave with you, My peace I give to you;
> not as the world gives do I give to you.
> Let not your heart be troubled, neither let it be afraid.
> — *John 14:27 NKJV*

THE END...
No!... The Beginning!
God's Realignment for Your New Assignment

Made in the USA
Monee, IL
17 March 2025

14085601R00063